Stars In You & Me

Evincepub Publishing

Published by

Evincepub Publishing

Nehru Nagar, Bilaspur, Chhattisgarh 495001

Website: www.evincepub.com
Email: publish@evincepub.com/ info@evincepub.com
Facebook: www.facebook.com/evincepub

ISBN: 978-93-5446-088-3

STARS IN YOU & ME

Shaheen Kazi

Acknowledgements

"I am an Author only when I have a Reader."

I want to dedicate this poem book to the following people:

My Readers: Wow!! It's always a fantastic feeling to write something for my Readers. After *Diary You & Me* and *Cupids Arrow*, I thought to write something different as my readers know I always write something about love. I am sure you guys have read many love poems, but this poem book is not about love. It's about you and me. I want to thank all my lovely readers for picking up my third poem book. Whatever I write, it's only for my readers. Massive Thank You to all who read my previous book and loved them too; your unconditional love and support have filled inside me the freshness and spirit to connect with you all through my words.

My Parents: Deep gratitude and thankfulness to my deceased parents Late ***Najma Kazi & Shaukat Kazi,*** for showering their love and blessings on me from above. Whatever knowledge I got from you both, today I am capable of penning down.

My Family: I am very thankful to the Almighty for every blessing in my life. My Star of my life, my fantastic lover in the form of my husband **'Rashad Kazi',** I can never find any words for you to thank you. You are the strong backbone of my life!

The Evince Publishing Team: This is my fourth book with you; I'm so fortunate to be part of your team again. You all changed my life completely. I honestly could not be more grateful for all of the opportunities that you have given me. The entire process would have been a waste if **EVINCEPUB** Publishing had not shown faith in this project. I extend my sincere gratitude to the whole team at Evincepub publishing to take this project past the finishing line and understand each requirement from start to end.

I can't wait to continue to impact lives with you guys. The best is yet to come!

I hope the readers enjoy the poem as much I had enjoyed while penning down!

"Writer only writes the book
but the Reader completes the book".

"I am born under the sign of Cancer,
Being romantic and caring honestly, it's not my fault."
-Shaheen Kazi

Contents

Introduction

Before you judge me for anything, I would like to tell all my readers that I am not an astrologer. But yes, I believe in the stars and I like reading about them. I have a deep interest in knowing zodiac signs because it helps me understand people more clearly. It makes my vision more explicit about the people whom I know.

All of us have relatives, friends and colleagues in our lives. But sometimes we all fail to understand each other, and the result turns into fight, arguments and sometimes even break-up. And after few years, one fine day, we think about that person and realize that we had loosened this beautiful relationship only for individual egos and follies. And now, apart from happy memories, we have nothing.

'Stars in You & Me' is a poetry book dedicated to personality. We are all born under an astrology sign; it is not a question of believing or not. The fact is that we are all tied to individual stars within us. In this book, I wrote 36 poems on the 12 signs of the Zodiac and how our (both man and woman) personality is different from each other or very compatible. Each zodiac sign has three sets of poems, one is about the Zodiac itself, and the other two is about the man and woman personality.

I had always written about love, feelings, intimacy and lust. Perhaps, in this book of poems, I wrote about the signs of the person's Zodiac, thoughts and behaviour under which its zodiac sign counts. My intentions are not to offend anyone's feelings while reading if you feel or disagree with a personality.

I hope you enjoy this beautiful poem book, and I hope all the flaws of our personality we overcome and try to understand each other's pattern of behaviour and our loved ones.

Shaheen Kazi

ARIES

ARIES

(Symbol: The Ram)

Mar 21–Apr 20

A – Adventurous Soul

R – Radiant Aurora

I – Impulsive

E – Enthusiastic

S – Strong & Independent Leaders

Aries

(Bold & Competitive)

I am the earliest rays of the Sun
I glow in my brilliant natural womb.
I express my passion endlessly
I carry the heavenly sparkles of eternity.

I'm the typical ram.
Very Impulsive
Very Enthusiastic

Aries arrives at the start of spring;
Full of passion with
Nice heartstrings to swing.

It is being numbered one on the Zodiac
Doesn't it matter where I'm at?
I can always love you
on the Moon and back.

Before I count from one to ten
Give me your attention
All over once again.

Being such an intrepid personality
I will be seen very rare
With such kind of lovely qualities
It is hard to find somewhere.
My courage encourages me the most

as my thoughts always;
flatters around like a welcoming host.

I am a born leader
with a determined achiever
I'm not sure I know that word,
'surrender',
I keep moving ahead
with a grin on my face,
in the intention of always
being remembered.

As I am aware, I will seal the magical moments
once and forever with smooth emotions.
Throw a pebble in
And then watch the dance of the ocean.

My daring tells the tale
Whichever steps I decide to take
Your views of me are pretty beyond the pale.

Whatever you do, never ignore me
And if you still my dear
I guarantee;
you will regret it no sooner or later.

If you suspect my calibre
I will prove you wrong
with great pleasure.

'Passion' and 'Sincerity' are the only key to my Star
My heart that walked with bitterness
comes back from very far.

I finally embrace my element
Just like my nature.
I was created by fire
With the warmness of
Passionate and desire.

♈

ARIES MAN

(Understanding Energies)

His birthday starts from March to April
He'll find roses all over the table.
He is quick when it comes to falling in love
That smile of Mars! – For this is his name,
this silent salvation from above
a weak spark of light that came.

His personality is not hard to decipher
whatever is running in his mind?
He will keep the situations quite
formal and lighter,
in better hours and much brighter.

He wants to feel needed, appreciated and loved
Sometimes all he wants is
to be talked to and;
a small amount of hug.

Perhaps he's got a rugged exterior
That's why he survives.
But real love is
how he genuinely stay alive.

If you are Jane
looking for Tarzan,
don't be the 'Twitter' chick on him
try to meet him in person.

There is no one more romantic or
more prepared to sweep you off.
He, too, had a spontaneous and fun side too
but,
being Aries, he seems to be serious at first with you.

But,
something you may not know
he is usually very shy.
Its better don't ask him the reason because,
even he doesn't know why? '

He is known for being generous and giving
The chant of joy in the spring;
come and touch his hand; it's a simple thing.

Being number one among the Zodiac
he may sound to you like a King.

Being a Battering Man
he never likes to quit.
If anyone ever underestimates
the Strength of its determination
they are sadly mistaken.

One of his biggest struggles
is being able to stay calm.

When he is slightly frustrated
He will be still a generous bomb
he has so much energy
that it can come out

as an explosion.

You can turn completely nuts
beware my friend,
but these are his emotions.

However, much he may seem
wide-eyed or naïve.
He is still not easy
for you to manipulate.

He never views anything in his
life as a mistake.

But for his own and his own love sake
sometimes he finds it difficult to confess.

Everything that happens in his life
Is it an experience?
On another sphere well,
it's human existence.

When he wants something
He will make it.
It may not be right
then and there;
but he will make it!

His mission to know
how much he cares.

Give him your time
and some understanding,
the roots of love for you
will always be there.

♈

ARIES WOMAN

(One Woman Army of the Zodiac)

She is a flower
out of the fairies' pockets.
From the new-born
zodiac locket.

Most of the time, she will be productive
But in an awkward mood,
she doesn't want to do anything!

An Aries Woman is like a
Superwoman.
What she wants,
she always gets in.
Don't ever try to mess
with her fanatic heart.
She moves in the firelight,
pensively apart.

Sometimes she is Impatient
and extremely energetic.
So sure, so sure, so connected
So pure, so pure, yet so
electric.

Being an Aries Woman
She enjoys freedom.
If you hold her tight
she may blow with the wind,
by giving you various reasons.

A bit of fame and fortune;
she no longer needed.
She may hold you again
to make you feel unlimited.

'Courageous'
is on the list as
one of her Strength.
Ah, but that kind of peace
rarely comes at length.

She is a woman with mind and spirit
to face any danger.
If you play with her emotions
she may forgive you only;
when she turns you into
a stranger.

The planet of passion rules her
Her story is one of the best actions,
where indeed she prefers.

She is a wildfire
She is not scared to work for her growth.
So she welcomes the unknown,
under the burning flames of an oath.

She has a difficult time relaxing
Her mind is always running,
always analysing.

Once the Aries woman
falls in love with you.
She shows her caring side
by fitting herself;
like a glove in blue.

She becomes, little possessive
when she sees *changes* a bit.
If she turns into fire,
under the roof, no guest shall sit.

Women ruled by the sign of Aries
Possess an impeccable sense of style.

Yet,

despite all this elegance
her heart remains like a child.

Aries Woman is the catch of Zodiac
They are romantic, passionate
and affectionate,
where in the world of girls
it's usually hard to get.
She will always embrace the Strength
and fight over the weakness
But she is not sure
she may even possess for sweetness.

Aries women are impressed by action or passion
If you are lucky enough,
you can be;
rewarded with a smile of

Satisfaction.

What you see is
what you get.
An intense physicality always attracts her
and her strength.

She's tough, sometimes gentle, and often rough
Don't step on her toes or
you'll get burned.

Born in April
she doesn't deserve sweets,
as she is much sweeter than maple.

The day when she walks into your kitchen
give her the mission and see,
how everything gets the label
you will only wonder,
what naughty tricks she put upon me?

Nothing is impossible for an Aries,

They're soldiers at heart.

TAURUS

TAURUS

(Symbol: The Bull)

Apr 21–May 21

T – Trustworthy

A – Aggressive

U – Undying Love

R – Romantic

U – Understanding

S – Stubborn

TAURUS

(Sensual & Creative)

I am a Taurus
Born with persistence and idleness.
I can't wait to give up on
any chance of greatness.

Enemies should never treat me lightly
because I am the soldier of God.
Friends value my love and affection
as they believe in each of my cause.

Such a lazy beast
no matter how much lightning struck me.

I still wouldn't move
But when I see my enemies
my hooves start stomping the ground
without any mixture of pedigrees.

You can call me a Space Cowboy
while I roll over my imaginary toys.

If I wish it, it will come
If I think it, it will be done
If I attempt it, it will be succeed
If I persuade it, it will prosper
If I just wait, then nothing will be proper.

I won't rest until my plan gets implemented
Being most stubborn,
sometimes my anger is laminated.

You see, my stubbornness is the only key
to interfere with absolute peace.
It is the short time during which
my misfortunes will cease.

Witty and practical, faithful and generous to friends
above the average still loves until the end.
Being a Taurus am solid as a rock,
like a pillar, guide
you will find me as a block.

I am the most dependable among the entire Zodiac
All zodiacs with 12 signs are unable to attack.
I am not fond of any changes,
I hate it more than anything else.

I am an intelligent, down to earth
Don't try to restrain me; I am the master of my birth.

I can deal with any situation without any direction of home
Like a rolling stone, like a complete unknown.

When life gets me down, I grab the nearest bowl
I dive into the bottomless drinks of life
to transform;
into a warrior soul.

I have an intense affliction for things
that arouses my senses.
Good food, good music and beautiful scenery
gives me immense happiness.

So much sloth and stubbornness together
become the recipe for my downfall at times.
But I know my needs; my sweet tumbleweeds
life sucks, sometimes.

I appreciate the loyalty in every friendship
and will never forsake any friend in difficult times.
But if you rub me in
a wrong way,
I can dreadfully play the enemy
and get you out of my way.

As being born in the merry month of May
A life without comfort is not a life for Taurus.
I see balloons and the women looking gorgeous
I can be your wonderful friend
even if the cupid warns me in chorus.

THE TAURUS MAN

(The Cowboy)

Taurus, Bull God; Strong and Proud
Sometimes he is lazy, quite often loud.

He could be stubborn,
but he's always with you, too!
By bringing flowers or gifts;
he can show how much he
adores you.

When he loves, he loves hard
He's no longer able to refuse once you have his card.

He holds on to fond memories stronger
than any other signs.
Just an old sweet song made new
by oozing through the pines.

Taurus Man is undoubtedly a lover
Not a warrior-but if you pressurize him
where it hurts;
he secretly grew into a
long-held grudge.

He is the man who does not believe
in the idea of love.
He is the man who believes
in the act of love.

He might be incredibly picky;
when it comes to a serious relationship

Once you are in,
he is sure not to soften his grip.

He is a control freak
But his style is unique.

Taurus Dudes are as reliable as hell
helpful super-sweet and heavy.
Spend time with them, and then you will know
how much they resemble;
like Tom & Jerry.

He is easy to go along guys
He reassures you by his act that is *his* flip side.
He is trustworthy,
only look at his love, filled with curves of the journey.

Their sense of humour is immature,
but they make it look cute every time
whenever it occurs.

Being the bull sign, he has quality
he won't sit lazily until;
he gets to the finish line.

He keeps everyone's inner regrets and secrets
that is the part of his sweetness.

A natural-born team leader
at times he becomes a teacher,
or he turns into an empty meter.

Sometimes people call him for advice
he acts as he is full of wise.
Sometimes he turns to give
a good dose of common sense,
because it is free of cost;
without any personal expense.

Being completely honest and
committed to their decisions.
He is neither afraid of waiting
in any situation;
or pass through any sensation.

He dares to wait for the results,
Though;
he silently checks his electrifying pulse.

He is well organized and handles it all well
He is a good finisher
that even he cannot tell.

He prefers to stay straightforward
rather than playing any games.
Bulls like all things beautiful,
be it at home or on any stage.

THE TAURUS WOMAN

(The Pillar of Affection)

Taurus woman personality
is an excellent balance of
sensitivity and toughness.

Hey,

She can give you love
in a package of abundance.

Taurus woman is gifted with high intelligence
and need an almost equal man.

She's straightforward and passionate
and constantly needs to be loved.
Her love can take you on the journey
from seven clouds above.

She is loyal but possessive and unbending
If her security has threatened,
her heart fills with hate
and trunks of weapons.

She could be dominant in some cases
But she also knows too,
To tie you up in her love laces.

In any relationship,
she will try to make it fulfilling
and fruitful experiences.

She is emotionally powerful,
and thus you can never see her
crumbling to pieces.

She likes things her way and
hates when others try to dictate.
She moves ahead freely,
with her thoughts of
tribe and fate.

She's never weary when she's in love
She feels comfortable around her partner
even though;
every turning life if it's a little too harder.

She is that independent,
focused, ambitious queen.
She is a boss; she can handle anyone
Do you know what I mean?

She has a soft, submissive side with a heart of gold.
Men have named beauty, but her Zodiac calls her bold.

She knows how to take care of a man.
She is spiritual, selfless and clearly understands.

Since Venus rules Taurus,
she is happy as a chorus.
She is a natural full of romance
her love creates in song and rhythm in her dance.

For her love should be always
eternal and magical.
As her heart fills
with the ocean of motions
with complete logic,
and sensual vibes of mystical.

Her kisses are steamy, and her eyes expressive.
But if you take her for granted,
You may find her aggressive.

Her zodiac birth is in
the house of planet Venus.
And thus she is the combination of
Pleasure, Love, Beauty
which will flow in every season.

♉

Taurus Takes Two Approaches' To Life -ALL or NOTHING-

GEMINI

GEMINI

(Symbol: Twins)

May 21–Jun 20

G – Gabby People loves to socialize
E – Experiment & Explore
M – Marvellously Practical
I – Imaginative and highly creative
N – Never consistent
I – Independent and hates to be tied down

GEMINI

(Social & Energetic)

It tends to be whimsical
I follow my pattern of the individual,
My attributes many times lead me to success,
I promise you; I never forget to make progress.

Being an Air Sign;
I have the intelligence and ability to think clearly.
The planet Mercury rules me
no need to take me for granted;
nothing vanishes from my memory.

Consider me one of the most
Bright signs of the Zodiac.

Due to some long frustrations
I sometimes, too, react.

Under the Sun, everything is the subject of fire for me
Pleasure is mine in constantly communicating with glee.

Without any exaggeration
I would like to say;
I am an encyclopaedia of sorts
in every kind of way.

By birth, I am Twins
We stay together like a pillow and hairpins.

The two-dimensional personality
keeps everyone enthralled.
Being so full of information on
anything and everything,
It is a pleasure to spend time
when you find me more than anything.

Everything within me feels perfect
However, the problem arises;
when I play the role of the suspect.

I might not be the best candidate
for a leadership role.
But whatever I possess,
I play it well, too well for a healthy soul.

Curious minds of the twins
I need to practice maintaining control.
That's where my trouble begins
when I leap from one thing to another;
my attention finds difficult
about (particular topic) to shower.

I am very energetic and enthusiastic about life
I absorb information and ideas
like a sponge in delight.

Of all the zodiacs
am an actual social butterfly.
And may not be bound by anyone
whoever passes me by?

My happiness and freedom are fundamental to me;
don't get me wrong, *O dear,*
I love to engage with the world around me.

Exploring new people and
be adaptable to any situation.
Sometimes it gives me restlessness
or piles of impulsiveness,
to come out from my imaginations.

There are times when my high energy attacks me
and gives me anxiety.
I fuss and fight;
then I lay forth my wings and
fly high finally.

My lack of consistency is perhaps
my greatest weakness.
I carry this unique ability to
taste the bunch of sweetness.

Gemini is notorious for flirting
but once they get bonded to someone.
They become blind;
to the whole world for one
and only deserving.

GEMINI GUY

(Dual Nature)

He is the ball of energy
switch shape like no other,
It is in his nature;
you won't find it in another.

His personality prevents him from being static;
You will always find him at the point of being a moving
fanatic.

He sometimes remains a mystery to others and
therefore often challenging to interpret.
Always in the company of suitors and friends;
as they love to be with him
in the form to celebrate.

Being an extrovert; no one will be a stranger to him
He is friendly and charming,
But at times, he becomes insulting.

He is a guy very talkative
and always likes to be the talk of the town.
He will roam freely without
wearing the blanket of shyness around.

Communication is the essential traits
of the Gemini Man.
A curious soul with an exploratory mind
He begins his journey, in which he likes to shine.

Being the Airy sign, he is highly adaptable
according to his whims and fancies.
You may find him in the part of almost everything;
whereas softly flirting around
with every woman weaving the covers of romances.

Always in the hunt for new experiences
continue to meet new people and
engage in different explorations.

He is exceptionally carefree like a child
if he didn't find things going right and fair,
he may sulk to extreme levels;
that can be wild and reasons for going anywhere.

Being a moody guy, he can be funny, light and vibrant,
He can be incredibly soft with beautiful combinations
of sentiments and silence.

To get the attention
anytime ready to lie;
But with the charismatic behaviour
his sparks remain high five.

Born with the versatile talent
with multiple of interest.
He never gets tired to show off
And use his qualities to the fullest.

Gemini Guy in love
is like a hard fish to hold;
Tend to move in different directions

It makes it him hard to stick with one
Enjoys being flirty and love to create some fun.

If Gemini Guy is in love with you,
they can be the most fun-loving partners
you will ever find it.

His demands in a relationship
needs a lot of space and independence.
But if he finds a clingy partner,
he will detest her presence
in the least among resemblance.

He is a Gemini Guy,
Born split into pieces.
He is two for one special
just like one buy one free
Without a doubt or
Without any question?

He lives in the present, it is assured;
that whatever moments is spend.

He makes it a memorable experience
right through to the end.

GEMINI GIRL

(The Fun side to Showcase)

Creativity is the most beautiful creation in her
this beauty she should undoubtedly prefer.

Being extrovert in nature
she is open-minded and accepts
all the milder feature.
Yes,
sometimes she constantly changes her interest
but she is unaware,
for someone can turn it out unimpressed.

She keeps trying a lot of things in her life,
as she has no idea where her passion arise.

Sometimes she becomes a very complex girl,
it becomes difficult for others
to understand her girly curls.

Gemini Girl personality is a good mixture
of being impulsive and caring.
Wandering in spirit and heart,
she will always be her beloved honey.

She is a romantic girl
and finds the unique ways
to charm and express her love.

Being very friendly she is a good friend
Can go to nurture her friendship
in any possible length.

Being a mutable sign,
always very dynamic and adjustable
in the pool of all divine.

She focuses on enjoying every moment of life
Craving for new things,
it's her favourite fundamental rights.

She believes in just passing her days
for a better future.
Each day she works to
make her present memorable and worth;
for a lovely picture.

She never stops learning
if she finds it interesting.
She can give you compliments
for the art you excel in.

She will push you to teach her
the various levels of anything.
No matter what,
she is ready to learn everything.

Gemini Girl in love can be very
easy going yet demanding.
She can be your cutest partner;
all you need to be understanding.

She fills with a lot of feminine touches
Her sweet face from brow to chin,
veiled with blushes.

Girl, of Gemini sign, has the personality
of talkative and being loud.
She doesn't like to be timid;
lonely amid the crowd.

Love to get attention but shy to express
Her divine appeal is unable to guess.

She gets highly attracted who
has the element of intelligence.
If she finds nothing,
she breaks the entire perimeter fence.

It is easy for her to ditch and move ahead
by clearing the way for a wedding.
She is the girl who is always
ready to make a new start,
even though if her heart is bleeding.

She can be introverted too
if she needed.

As she loves her lonely space
whenever her mood demands,
about another time and place.

If anyone of you wants a Gemini lady
to fall in love with you.

Then become a good listener;
and accept her through.
Most essential to understand
her mutual nature,
She is God's creation
of a nice fun-magnet mixture.

The Twins inside the Gemini's mind fight each other between what's right and what's Wrong.

CANCER

CANCER

(Symbol: Crab)

Jun 21–Jul 20

C – Caring & Kind-Hearted
A – Accommodating & Extremely Helpful
N – Nurturing & Family Oriented
C – Clingy but Self-Sufficient
E – Emotionally Responsive
R – Romance Beautifully

CANCER

(Intuitive & Energetic)

I am a moonchild;
Thus, my mood is wax and wane.
The Moon is my ruler,
and my symbol for crab
is not inferior to a jeweller.

Let's not deny this,
I am the most emotional sign among all zodiacs.
The flip side of mine is,
am not always the first to express.

I tend to be the perfect blend of 'shy' and 'sweet.'
And on the other side,
wild and crazy.
I tend to dive into the pool of emotions often,
you will find me being happy and
gloomy at any other moment.

I have a heart of gold, and I proudly wear it on my sleeves.
I love to help people,
even once they were my formidable core enemies.

I am not known to hold grudges for too long,
I would somewhere forgive you by plucking all the thorns.

People like to come to me and find solace in my nurturing
nature and kindness.

I am blessed with a sharp memory and
love to tell you many old stories.

But, certain things, I don't say to anyone
Shhh….SOME SECRETS!

Have to be preserved and kept hidden forever.
Being a water sign,
I have an intuitive power able to use it broadly;
it feels like a plenteous shower which kicks me strongly.

I am not open to everyone
but when I do,
it is good fun to have me around.

Like a crab, I often avoid confrontation by hiding in my shell.
Preferring not to get into a heating battle;
sometimes it hurts me as well.

Sometimes, I lose to express my feelings directly,
even if I read you correct!

I am a caring and indeed a symbol of LOVE;
particularly with my loved ones.
Being faithful, loving, protective,
These qualities are inside me, where I shine.
To be with you,
I am always ready to break any thin or fine lines.

I am very perceptive of other people's emotions;
as I feel they are not alone in the drift of the ocean.
Very receptive to their needs

psychic and intuitive is in my nature;
after all, this is my one and only unique feature.

An immense amount of love to give
that is my only strength.
Ah, but sometimes it causes me to come across as
clingy, needy and possessive at length.

I like to demonstrate
my feelings and longing,
Being very expressive;
Is the spirit of my belonging?

I love receiving gifts, especially when it has
the element of SURPRISE!
Even on earth,
I feel like I am walking in paradise.

I hate to be in the middle of any argument
and stay away from home.
My personality goes better with classic things
even if I live in a mansion or might even, in the dome.

As my love holds for them;
while my spirit swirls and my heart sings.
My dreams are endless to dream about
of any queen or any romantic king.

Moon is the moody planet of mine,
Cancer is the cardinal water sign.
Water symbolizes depth and wavering behaviour,
My eyes are always in the hope of any saviour.

I am known for my commitments,
emotional intensity and parenting instincts.
I will be one in your team
who knows and keeps all your secrets.

You won't ever regret having me in your life.
Moon controls me, and this relationship is deep
and sharp like a knife.

The embalm of Cancer is CRAB,
No wonder I am named crabby!

In a swift, I return to my shell.
It is not a big deal for me, though
because this 'box' is my second home
where I secretly lye.

Being Cancer,
am blessed with vast imaginations.
I can transform a 'word' into a story
as being known to be imaginative geniuses,
to bring out the most resounding glory.

Through poems and writings
I feel delighted to
ooze out my feelings and share.
To an extent,
I possess intense creative energy
I engage in the art to express myself
to build the tower of memory.

Cancer is the most sensitive sign,
think with the heart and less use the mind.

Concerned for safe and faithful connection
very caring and loyal.
Always ready to toast the glass
with the master of the house,
without a doubt, I can even die for my spouse.

It's not easy to love Cancer because they love deeply
in every manner.
Cancer needs deep love from someone
who can complete them to live in a fairy-tale world,
created by that *special* one.

They have got a blind spot for the one they love
intensely,
And they'll forget everything
when it matters to them entirely.

CANCERIAN MALE

(Highly Empathetic & Sensitive Beings)

Being related to the water element
depth runs deep inside his veins.
He is very tender and easily gets bruised
sometimes he will stare and stare;
no wonder still he will look confused.

He gets hard on the outside
with a bunch of sensitivities inside.
A family man loves to please his partner
in thrifty, moods shift all the time.

Motherly instinct is in abundance in his nature
acting on its best is his behaviour.
Extremely sensitive
and vigilant of everyone's needs.
In the smile of his loved ones where the crab man heart
'beats'.

He is always dependent on his friends and family
That doesn't make him weak.
Only these are his usual emotional outbursts
where he keeps himself last,
but always prefer to give them a start.

It is challenging for him to live in the present
He finds it hard to forgive or forget,
as his mind sometimes intend.

He, too, has a funny side inside his fragile heart
If he feels comfortable around,
his funny-loving person can pop out.

Being always dedicated towards his duties
Under each situation, without hesitation,
he will reply to you coolly!

Cancerian Man is extremely chivalries soul
Very sensitive and get easily wounded
from any silly troll.

Being intuitive is one of the
the Cancer Man's most fundamental traits.
He believes in his vibes,
and loves to stay far away
from any kind of debates.

Being supportive, sentimental, moody,
family-oriented and loyal
includes all these qualities.
It may seem, for some, lacklustre/pleasant.
But that's his personality.

Always live under the shade of nostalgic time
Very traditional yet loves to hear praises,
with the sugar-coated rhymes.

Patience walks hand in hand
with a Cancer Man personality.
He may never leave you midway
even though you're in pain at the wrong time,
you shall find his stay.

Highly versatile and social in needed situations
Lazy at times and
highly unpredictable.

If he acts weird lately
give him some time.
No matter what
he will be alright, as you will
always be on his list as a prime.

Being romantic,
it is easy for him to fall in love, head over his heels.

Cancerian man in love
can be a giver of another extent
where his heart kneels.

He will always try to be perfect
one-hundred per cent.
He will prove to be your best prince charming
Always ready to snuggle in you;
as you will be only his feminine.

He only expects the same level of inclination
and involvement in return.
Your love will never bestow the Sun
as it will keep his flames highly burn.

Due to extreme emotions
he might show a bit of jealousy and possessiveness.
His personality is a nurturing one
and thus the relationship;
continuously blooms in excessiveness.

You will never find him giving up on love so easily
He only needs the same kind of dedication from you
Finally.

CANCERIAN FEMALE

(Essence of Romance)

She is the daughter of the Moon
The way she moves,
on the nightingale tune.

She is the ocean of love where she floats
in the waves of romance.
To attract her, you need to be
considerate and intimate in any chance.

Once you find her, you will be sailing your boat
in the life of Atlantic.
Where your story will be;
quiet and sometimes steamy romantic.

Moon is her ruling planet,
but never dare to take her love for granted.
She is a mixture of passion and calmness
everything bows to her beauty,
her love for you will always remain flawless.

She is highly willing and persistent
But if disturbed or provoked;
your complete charm can be non-existent.

She needs a man
who can accept her strange mood swings.
Give her the wings of love to fly with
a few of her favourite things.

Cancerian woman has a heart of gold
Beautiful inside out, which makes anyone bold.
She laughs easily and sacrifices a lot.

Her moodiness is something she can't control.
She's a fighter and a keeper,
once you fall for her, it's hard to leave her.

Her hidden talent is reading people
Raise a glass of goodness and evil.
Sometimes her real problem starts by
loving the wrong person hard,
either she ends her life in the thoughts of junkyards;
or in any graveyard.

Her Zodiac is the first water sign
and the Moon rules the Cancer woman;
endowing her with brilliant intuition and creativity.
She is deeply intuitive;
which causes her longevity.

She might fail to give you any explanation
But sooner or later;
she definitely will be proven right.
It's not about her being judgemental,
it's all about her inner emotions
and the bunch of institution style.

If ever you criticize her,
she can take it personally very well!
She can never forget as she too doesn't know
till where her bound is?

Even she might fail to express.

Like her, understand her, but don't ever underestimate her
She may surprise you one day when you had least expected,
It won't be easy for you to prefer.

Cancerian woman is sensitive-very sensitive
You will be surprised to know not only for her;
but for others need to as well.

Her lucky stone is a moon pearl.
Wherein her star jewels.

One of the Zodiacs most compassionate and
the loving woman you will find.
When she says she's going to do something,
believe she's going to make it happen
back in a little while.

She is a genuinely valuable addition
to any team or community.
The feeling of a mother is at home,
in every step of absolute eternity.

You can name her true magician
behind the scenes;
in building a prop or inside the
kitchen.

She prefers working with her hands
and researching with it.

Cancerous females are homely goddesses
which connect easily.
And it won't be easy for you to separate
with her pleasingly.

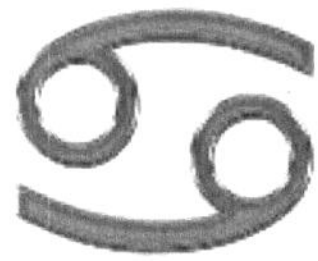

Just like the Moon,
Cancer shines in times of darkness.

LEO

LEO

(Symbol: Lion)

July 23–Aug 22

L – Lion-Hearted for your courage
E – Easy-going personality like a breeze
O – Outstanding in each & every way

LEO

(Fiery & Self-Assured)

As the leader of the pack
It is hard for me to turn my back.
About anything shouts my attention;
each time to conquer is my greatest invention.

I am the cynosure of all eyes
as I walk with my head held high.
It won't be easy to ignore me
without covering your white lies.

I believe this world is my kingdom and that
where I meant to rule it.
However,

this rise can give me arrogance and haughtiness.
But that is the task for me;
for not letting the pride come into my way of happiness.

Richness and fame inspire me the most
Even though I won't admit it,
I will cheer my lifestyle in a very high roast.

Being Leo, I am highly competitive and stubborn
But I also have a soft heart to boot.
Always being confident that's the reason;
challenges can never threaten me in any seasons.

Being the leader of any team
I am always there from the shut stable
to the frozen stream.

I am benevolent and always ready to go out of my way,
will get the result of the success is my aim
without even caring for night and day.

My hot temper is the thing for me to fear the most
Losing control can cause significant damage,
any relationship will bid a farewell into a black hole.

I aim for success in my life
pouring the fuel of ambitions, wealth
and luxury style.

Being very confident whatever I do,
Always remains the centre of attraction whenever
I pass through.

Let's, face it
I am highly independent but,
I prefer to have an audience.
Being loyal to my loved ones in the same way like;
every day how the Sun comes.

I thrive off new situations, dramas
and need excitement in my life.
If I don't have them,
I create some to enjoy the crazy drive.

I am likeable because of my substantial warm heart
I am also headstrong and stubborn,
without staying apart.

Tolerant of other people and their views
but no tolerance for anyone.
Who does want to change *you*? (Leo)

The lion in me is controlling and domineering
but never nasty.
Sometimes I turn into a
bad, bad daddy.
I treat others as equals;
despite controlling the band of happy people.

Being a lion,

I always like to remain active and engage in fun activities.
I want to party hard;
in the manner to hold every card.

Who don't love compliments?
Me too is the one among all.
There's one thing I've got to confess,
I boom this tagline, *"Dress to impress"*.

Always enjoys the company of elegant, rich and beautiful people
Likes to be surrounded by beautiful objects;
as much as possible.

You have no idea,
how much I dislike being in the company of
dull and lazy people.
Spending an extra moment with them
for me;
it's an act illegal.

I can hurt you by my wounded, sharp words
When I pay too much attention to harp nerds.
So better stay away,
when you don't hear my familiar chord;
Of course, your voice can easily be ignored.

I want all things nice, but if I don't get it
My tempers flare into giant size.
'Exploring' and 'Experimenting' are my passion,
It will always remain inside me like a *classic fashion.*

LEO LION

(Lion)

A Leo Man is very boisterous
Leo Traits in male make them
very charming and self-confident.
Always surrounds himself with people;
who can add a special touch of compliment
tall as a steeple.

Sometimes someone can see him
as self-centred too.

He has materialistic likings as he had a heart of gold
Well, he doesn't know much, but it is a fact
he, too, has different layers of moulds.

Enthusiasm is at the peak
when he is working on something.
Being very smart in work,
he believes in organizing between
red, white and blue shoe strings.

It's not a big deal to see a Leo Man
with a daily planner;
his work appears like an actual banner.
He has agendas and targets ready
before even their morning starts;
his work requires no knowledge on the paper
or any other chart.

He is always the Star of his group
glittering better than others.
Being with someone automatically;
takes all the charge of being the
man of the moment is the lifer at large.

You can name him as Mr Perfectionist
in whatever he put his hands and mind.
Indeed, he will come out with the flying colours,
leaving everyone a thousand miles behind.

He is ruled by Sun
and thus he is seen as highly energetic
and charismatic in one.
Though being symbolized by a lion,
he is a kind-hearted guy.
He is a natural performer without any limelight or
without feeling shy.

He has a line which not everyone
in their long list of friends can cross.
He does go overboard in sharing his lives
and moments with people,
but are very selective about with whom he shares his
thoughts.

Being a fire sign, Leo man has a lot of passion
when it comes to love someone.
He is the guy with a series of love affairs;
he always picks the opportunity like
running up and down the stairs.

To match up with the toughness of Leo
A robust companion is needed.
Leo man is a bold lover,
His affair can be pretty heated.

LEO LIONESS

(Lady born under the sign of fire)

She is the Queen,
her soul is Royal.
Just shake your hands with her,
as the fans always stay Loyal!

You can't mistake a Leo lady
when she breaks into a room.
All eyes turn towards her as
She can be name a goddess of gloom.

When she talks, people gravitate forward to listen,
When she dresses;
She can hear the bells of various hearts
from a very far away distance.

Leo Woman is socially aware of how to act,
She's the ideal hostess without a single fact.

Despite being,

Charming and stylish in manner
She will be greeting around
along the rollers in the hair;
with the attitude of 'doesn't even matter.

For some, it will be funny, or for some, it will be childish
Forgetfully, she will perform herself like a genuine stylist.

Enjoys pampering, manicures, pedicures,
full body massages and find a milk bath very relaxing.
Anything that gets a purring for her is perfect;
always excited to try different beauty masks,
until she tags it correct nicely.

Typically, it is easy to pick a Leo dame in the crowd
she's the one with the loudest and hardest chuckle.

It's a feline symbol ruled by the Sun centre of the universe
She always grabs the attention and adds inside her purse

Sometimes you will see her claws out
if you stepped outside the line.
So handle her carefully like a red glass of wine.

Leo women are warm and energetic
at expressing her passion.
She sparkles her world with a whole fashion.
A relationship with Leo women will always be fun
She thinks to introduce change and excitement,
as she hated repetition when it's already; been done.

Yeah, at times, the guys will feel her love playing
like a fire,
inflame the flames in the furnaces of desires.

There's a fire in her
If loved correctly, she will warm your entire home.
If abused,
She will burn it down in fumes.

She has been mix with hellfire and holy water
whichever flavours you taste.
It depends on how you will treat her
And what you will get.

Leo refuses to compromise with their standards. If they are putting in 100%, why should Do they settle for less?

VIRGO

VIRGO

(Symbol: The Virgin)

Aug 23–Sept 22

V – Very fussy for perfection
I – Intelligent & Analytical thinker
R – Reliable person who you can count on
G – Groomed in thoughts and conduct
O – Observant & take mental notes

VIRGO

(Practical & Logical)

A carefully prepared chocolate fondant is what
describes Virgo the best,
Soft and *Subtle* on the outside;
but still, never reveals what can be inside?

I do not get swayed by emotions
which is great!
When the time comes, I come out with
large explosions on the clean slate.

Just like the chocolate that oozes out from the
fondant.
Amount of time,
I have to deal with such nonsense.

I am always meticulous and analytical
I take great care of ensuring perfection as typical.
Organizing things in the right way is my birthright,
to spot the tiniest faults is my ability to describe.

I don't quickly lose my temper
but when I do,
I cleverly divert my attention towards my passion
where,
I can surrender.

I do not like to be bossy
But I love to work as a team.
Being a perfectionist is my only theme,
from the first till the last extreme.

Hypocrisy, I genuinely detest in any form of shape
my vocal is heard strong enough,
at expressing without the route of being an escape.

Somewhere I carry the elephant's memory
which is enforceable for me to forget.
My enemies' wonder how do I remember,
even after years, they silently regret.

Observation and Awareness is my subtle gesture
I don't miss a thing; even it's a crease on the bed or
news from the broken weather.

Am an incredibly organized Virgo
I'm not particularly eager to live in the fantasy world.
And thus when I organize my life;
I intend to act upon even where the dim tides come hurled.

Sometimes the detail of my organization and
attention makes me a lit bit fussy.
Little moan at imperfection
low down my spirits, hussy.
Others are always reliable on my practical nature
I usually make plans and think of a better future.

Having the intelligence button in me
always curious to learn new things and
I grew my information every moment about the sea.

Most of the time, I prefer routine
but that doesn't mean;
I believe what I see the scene or read in any magazine.

I don't care for idealism, and my goals are well-rooted.
You will never find me relax;
until my work is well executed.

When others enjoy and have fun
I will be drowning in my work.
Sitting idle makes my mind
entirely into messy shirk.

Being a Virgo, I love to be in order
I collect things and keep them within me.
No hanky-panky is allowed or entertained on my border.

Rarely, I lose stuff and always keep things
in the right place.
I can keep a secret, something in style and grace.

I have an analytical mind
where I can see things from
black and white.

Ruled by Mercury
is the symbol of intelligence.
I know to show the world a 'Happy Face',
Does the Virgo child bless with that grace?

VIRGO MAN

(Hard to impress)

The best problem solver in her life
Lucky will be
Who will be his wife?

He is the true, genuine guider in every proper way
Very ground to earth, it's a price what he pays.

He is mutable, and thus he gets along with many people
But he let very few to come near his way.
It makes it significantly harder for others to guess,
what he will bring in his coffee tray
without creating any mess?

He loves to work in a clean
and organized environment.
Thus, he stays away from clumsy and
unhygienic harassment.

He adds his maximum efforts in everything
hardly he can sit idle and do not do anything.
Anyone can find him stimulative with something,
even if it is too much or not at all for nothing.

He always demands perfection and
correct in his ever first try.
He never gets scared with the failures
Endlessly,
He will triumph over the power of fright.

To sum up the Virgo man in a single word
it would be 'PRACTICAL'.
He sees stuff that they are without sugar coating or
without any social voting.

He is a down-to-earth and hardworking guy
who sees no need for unnecessary
outpourings of emotions
to please the blue sky!

Virgo Man's personality is an excellent mixture
of efficiency and deep care.
They keep their affairs private and
expect the same from their co-pilot.

He is a man of hard work, intelligent
and adventurous.
He is calculative, yet somehow,
follows his heart in different eras
of being childish.

Being sensitive, he doesn't allow too many people
to peep into his lives.
Being very confident about his thoughts
thus he sometimes lacks to take advice.

He sticks to his plans
without a doubt; he sounds man of words.
Any alteration in his task,
Are you sure? He will ask.

The most intense and loyal lover, he is
For him, love is not a temporary affair,
it's a long investment and commitment
without a doubt, he declares.

It's not easy for Virgo Man to fall for you
they need a strong lover who can get into his heart
bit-by-bit like single dew.

The most loyal signs of all zodiacs
you may find.

He finds it hard to fall in love, but once when he is in love
The way he shows his affection no one can ever imagine.
How much he got something to shower his sweet
expressions.
If you believe it, yes, it does happen.

♍

VIRGO WOMAN

(Beauty & Brains)

She is someone where you have to discover
Don't expect her to be a desperate lover.
She doesn't divulge much to anyone quickly,
A Virgo woman is relatively picky.

She will tell you precisely what she thinks
Or,
will remain silent.
Be aware! They can be sometimes
unspeakable violent.

The Virgo woman is the actual perfect blend of
Beauty and *Brains.*
Old times will never harm you
if your charm remains.

Described by the Virgin's sign
a Virgo woman is humble and reserved;
never tries to break any thin line.

She can hide her feelings extremely well
which makes her very hard to read.
Only people close to her know
what she is going through-you will find her emotions
like moonlight covered in snow.

She blessed with beauty in all ways
She is never tired to take all the praise.

A virgin goddess, pure, simple mind
lofty goals to touch the sky.
There can be only one problem,
what to do?
She can't forgive the lie.

People adore her abilities
as her bag is full of responsibilities.
She is humble, reserved, but
she is not a prude woman.

She wants to be forever
whenever her intense, romantically earthy sign arouse.
Her love is poetry in motion
and her,
fantasies capture an image of devotion.

She will be a great friend
unless faced with betrayal.
Then she will forget you
like if ever you existed as well.

She is a lady with high standards,
and kindness dwells inside her heart.
She doesn't demand perfection
she only desires catchy, honest direction.

Virgos are certainly not a follower. Virgos are a creator, and they create their ways.

Hashtags of Your Zodiac:

ARIES

#AlwaysBusy

TAURUS

#WaitingForMyFood

GEMINI

#DoubleTheTrouble

CANCER

#HowToUnloveSomeone

LEO

#MyPlaylistBetterThanYours

VIRGO

#MyMiddleNameIsSimple

LIBRA

LIBRA

(Symbol: The Scales)

Sept 23–Oct 22

L – Love & Beauty captures their heart
I – Indecisive & Judgemental
B – Balance is what they seek
R – Restful & strives for peace
A – Alluring Charm

LIBRA

(Fair-Minded & Diplomatic)

'L' for Libra
'L' for Lazy
I make everything calm for me
that's why I love all my
besties.

My Zodiac has the element of air,
which makes me calculative and fair.
Natural cleverness of the simple humour
on the surface;
It makes my Zodiac awesome, like the growing size of
rumour
Sometimes it is truth, or sometimes it is dare.
I am very good at balancing love
Not in the manner of somersaulting on a beam or,
walking on a tight rope.
But holding things somewhat to shape;
the relations in building with hope.

The most charming sign of the entire Zodiac
Up and down, front and rear.
Venus always rules me over beauty, arts, passion and
pleasure,
am always in the opportunity to smell these kinds of leisure.

Venus makes me a beautiful lover
emblem of scales makes me accurate, genuine fairer.

Justice of plates makes me balance
the highs and lows on various challenges.

I become go bonkers when it comes to romance
as the planet of love, Venus rule and dance.
Everyone in love can get a little crazy,
but being Libra is something different, *baby!*

To be Libra, to be born with all the charms
Being charming and flirtatious,
my welcoming personality; reaches out to others.

Like a giant brainy sponge;
I soak up all the thoughts
and knowledge around me.
I dislike disputes and confrontations
Instead,
I prefer to listen to others.

Language is essential for me
it is always in the control of my words and care.
I am always aware of my actions
for not hurting you or others.

Everyone's side of the story is always important to me.
Listening to everyone doesn't mean
any naughty tricks you can put upon me.

Honey and sugar, I bet it is so classy
Half of me am good, but the other half am nasty.

The hardest thing for me is to decide
sometimes I fail to speak for myself, and I silently hide.
Due to multiple personalities makes me unreliable
it breaks me many times and leaves me
unrecognizable.

I know how to please both the sides
So that,
in the end, I cheer up on the roller coaster rides.

♎

LIBRA MAN

(Love & Pleasure)

Venus governs the man of Libra
This planet of love and enjoyment is between us.
He is the natural giver when it comes,
to give to one's loved ones like a running river.

He is the provider of extreme pleasure, unearthly love
and a balanced approach towards life.
He is never in eagerness to make
the pretty girl, his wife.

He is the lavish spender in all ways
whether he can afford it or not?
He will always try his level best,
even on his rainy days.

To be in the good books of Libra Man,
you need to show your pleasant personality.
He is a very social guy
with some fun-loving qualities.

He always loves to keep a balance
between their lives and thoughts.
He loves to speak about his ideas
only to whom,
who is interested in hearing him out.

He can be a team player but fails to be a leader
Because it is hard for him to make a decision prompt.
As he is genuinely not a heartbreaker;
whereas, sometimes, his heart gets stomped.

He always makes sure not to hurt others with his words
thus he speaks in a balanced manner.
Whatever the situation he comes across,
for him, the circumstances
will never matter.

The most neutral and unbiased man
you will come across.
For him to look at every side, hear every individual.
Before coming to any conclusions,
his soul tells him what is visible.

Libra Man is sensitive but very masculine
He is a very balanced person
You can never imagine.
Being very charming and intelligent
He is the man without a sign of arrogance.

Libra Man in love is a beautiful sight to see
He is known as a trustworthy, profound lover.
He still finds it hard to show his inner feelings as
he lacks the quality of opening up with feathers.

Does it become challenging for a Libra man?
To make up his mind whom he is seeing?
He takes his own sweet time to be sure,
before of all the things.

He is a man of soft tonal personality
He is the man who always looks for stability.
He never rushes to fall in love
But when he does, he acts very patiently.

♎

LIBRAN WOMAN

(Dream woman)

A Balance woman can never stand by a hobbyist
She's willing to try anything until she finds her
Mr Perfectionist.

Freedom is her necessity
turning away from negative people
is her,
lovely secret recipe.

She is the friendly queen of balance and fairness
Her heart and leadership are selfless.
She's intelligent, gentle and
her beauty is ageless.
Sometimes she wonders how the face of love changes
by turning few pages.

She's not a fighter, but a diplomat for
inner peace and happiness.
Flirts in a million ways
Swifts,
like air from place to place.

Infatuated with sweets and luxury
comforts come to her instantly.
There comes the altitude of talent
She can persuade anybody,
with her sweet tongue violence.

Belonging to the planet of beauty,
she is the freelancer towards her duty.
Libra is a sign controlled by Venus
Libran female is complete '*Genius*'.

Romanticism can dominate Libra
She finds harmony with her lover.
She is proud to be loved and charm
And dedicated to her chosen one
with her heart warm.

She is the rigorously unbiased lady
and painfully honest at times,

Indeed, these are its beauties.

Her temperament is incredibly flirty
But *love* and *trust* are something she takes very seriously.

Her confidence is great
Her abilities have a lot of weight.
Fair, loving, thoughtful and kind
Every man desires, but it's hard to find.

Well known as the mediators of the Zodiac
Many men search endlessly across the world.
Looking for the perfect match
with the Libra woman,
she gives herself to that one whom she finds
his soul is human.

Libra is a zodiac sign that likes to communicate with others.

SCORPIO

SCORPIO

(Symbol: Scorpion)

Oct 23–Nov 21

S – Secretive type of personality
C – Calmness like a sea
O – Original with innovative ideas
R – Resentful when angry
P – Possessive in relationship
I – Inspiring to others
O – Obey their hearts

SCORPIO

(Passionate & Resourceful)

'Scorpios' own the word mysterious
Everything about me spells mystery
To keep secrets within me
Is my upper level of mastery?

I may seem cold-blooded on the surface,
but extremely emotionally underneath.

I belong to the Zodiac aquatic element
It's funny when people give me fire compliment.
At first glance,
for some, I look like a fire sign
But below, I am layered with a lot of emotional sides.

I, too, have levels and am known as the enigma of the Zodiac
I, too, have mastered the art of telling you a riddle
in such a way that I bet,
you won't be able to justify if it's real or there's a gap in the middle?

I am introverted and keep my feelings only to myself
I tend to have a barrier for my inner thoughts ahead,
a shelf over the shelf to sense the comfort of the bed.

I am blessed with two celestial forces
Mars and Pluto are my two only soldiers which
makes me powerful in all sources.

The emblem of Scorpio is the Scorpio
and that is no mistake.
It's a sign of beauty even if,
I lose my tail; it will grow prompt like a mystery.

I am focused
I am competitive
I just go for what I want it.
I am brave
I am bold
I am a brave-hearted Scorpio.
To deal with any insane stranger,
I am always ready to deal with various kinds of danger.

I obey my heart when I am in love
Loyal, strong, protective, gentle is my
commitment till the end.
I can deal with any harsh obstacle,
no matter what comes in my way to extend.

Faith and integrity are my symbols of
ferociously and loyally.
I expect the same from my partner,
and little;
add-on to treat me like royalty.

Don't mistake my envy for a joke.
If you do something wrong, you will be
paid in an absolute choke.

When it comes to commitment
am not only loyal to my friends and lovers,
am also dedicated to my enemies as well!

I never forgive, nor do I forget
Sooner or later, you will realize
there's no room for regret.

I am the most enigmatic and secretive sign
I just want to win and rule that's only
my aim you will ever find.

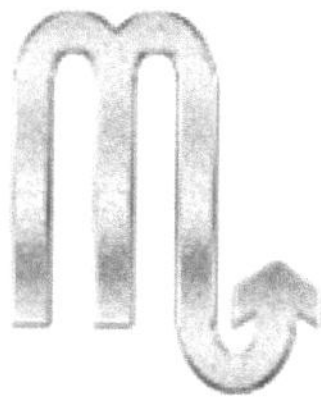

SCORPIO MAN

(One Smooth Guy)

He remains quiet and works in silence
He can act moody in various circumstances
He deals patiently with any situations,
only to ease his rising frustrations.

Wearing hard shells on the exterior is the cover of his protection.
Deep down, he has an intense personality
that only comes out in front of the
correct human.

Apart from being unforgiving and hardworking
He has a very calm side, too, just like stillness water.
He is never afraid to speak up nor
bottle up things,
friends and family are always on his precious strings.

Scorpio man is very spontaneous and always on
search to do new things in life.
He loves to be in power and look forward
to build the most beautiful and blessed tower.

His work ethics are strong, and he always climbs
the stairs of success in any blow of wind
or in any noisy storm.
Like all other water signs,
Scorpio man, too, has a curious mind.

His hard work leads to the direction of success
He is a fixed sign with highly
ambitious and independent.

He is fearless and never shy to
speak out with his heart and mind.

Scorpio guy personality is very complex
Being the born winner;
he always rises and sparkles like a duplex.

He is sharp, a quick thinker and
good at solving puzzles.
These are just a few qualities, and there are more to impress
once you step in his outstanding priorities.

He is the man who doesn't possess the
power to forgive and forget.
He keeps boiling his rage, and at
the perfect time, he takes his revenge.

He is a man of complete maturity and intensity
He is full of desire and passionate
for various melodies.

A Scorpio man in love
can be a little insecure at times.
Although he has an intense and pure passion
Sometimes in love, he demands of being
Suspicious or possessed.

He doesn't believe in playing around
with your feelings,
He is very straightforward when it comes
for commitment in anything.

It's not easy for a Scorpio guy
to handle the loss of his beloved.
He can never let go so easily
after investing his emotions so much
in her beloved deeply.

A Scorpio man can go to
any length, any depth,
to protect the charm of his relationship.

He is not a man who looks
to crush out easily
from his wonderful love trip.

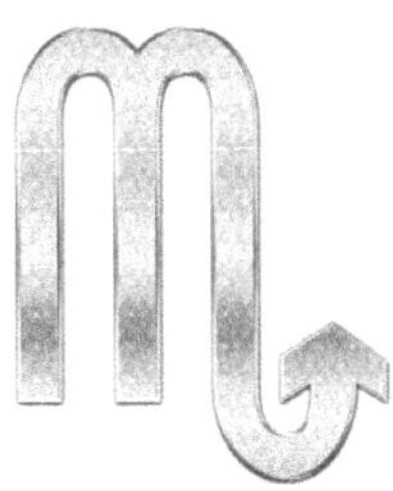

SCORPIO WOMAN

(Sex Goddess)

Scorpio women are the true *Queens*
of the underworld.
She's fascinated by all things;
spooky and mystical.
And never shy of her extreme or heavy
existence.

She is under the eight zodiac signs
Which is it all about?
Sex, death and rebirth process.

One should never take the Scorpio women lightly.
As she is good enough to ignore the issues,
which bothers her unnecessary.

She is the woman of mystery
she never seems to age
but,
magnificently increases in the direction of
wisdom and maturity.

Deep and magnetic, she's sharp and feminine.
She can read people and their intentions;
in everyone at one time.

Passionate and determined observant, she remembers all the fine details.

She craves deeper connections
to bind her to the depth of affection.

She wears strength and darkness equally well
She is the girl who will be always
half goddess and mind-you even, 'Half Hell'.

She can be your worst enemy or most loyal friends
Sometimes she likes to pretend.

She flows like hot lava
Once,
she has done with the useless drama.

She looks hot and intense
She is a goddess of passion.
When she cares about a man,
She'll love it to the end.

She knew herself to be a sex goddess.
She is known to lust and high sexual hottest.

She is demanding, but only
because;
she deserves the best.

Her genuine personality is hard to discern
she tries to keep it confined to a secret.

She loves the mystery she emits to others
Sweet or sour,
it depends on how you treat her,

Silence is the secret weapon of Scorpio.

SAGITTARIUS

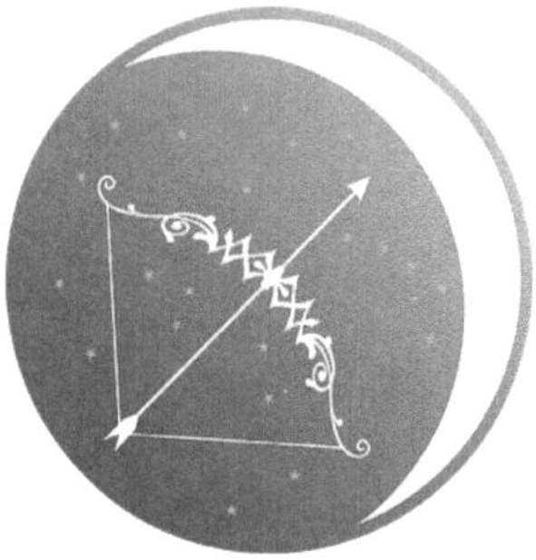

SAGITTARIUS

(Symbol: Archer)

Nov 22–Dec 21

S – Seeks for Attention

A – Adventurous Spirit

G – Great Friend

I – Intellectual

T – Thrill to chase

T – Takes no crap

A – Agrees to please folks

R – Restless in real

I – Impatient

U – Understanding

S – Sarcastic

SAGITTARIUS

(Adventurous & Funny)

If Zodiac were theme park rides
Sagittarius would be the hair-raising
white-knuckle rollercoaster slide.

I belong to the zodiac fire element
the archer is my natural ornament.

I am known to be a wild zodiac child
nothing can come in between of my liberty
when I am free;
my hearts flatter with a smile.

Philosophy is an attraction to me.
The arrows point to the sky-high
though sometimes;
my objectives are too distant from my vision
Every minor detail is my major decision.

Always being adventurous and free spirits
I live my life on my own merits.
I am an explorer,
I love to travel from one place to another.

Socially am active everywhere
still,
my friends take kindly to my attitude
too much alike –

Just and Fair!

Yes, I am fun, free spirit and
drawn to life thrills.
But I have intense dreams
tons of ambition and
goals to fulfil.
When I feel something deeply
It can tear my world apart.
I am a Fire sign
So yes,
my temper gets a little 'heated.'
But I forgive equally easily,
even if I had been mistreated.

Fortunately, I have the blessings of Jupiter
that seems to guide me correctly.
There is always a beaming smile on my face
maybe for some, I look like a stupider.

Reading and Writing
I enjoy it the most.
These are my secret tools where I
rarely like to boast.
When problems rock my boat
I become edgy and insecure.

I'm not particularly eager
to take the counsel from others.
To figure out and get the perfect curve,
I am aware of what actions will be well deserved.

Only one thing I hate the most
if am keep waited.
He or she, in my opinion,
Sooner or later will be faded.

My embalm is an
archer which suits my wild nature.
Good companies and friends around
It always gives me sweet pleasure.

SAGITTARIUS MAN

(Free bird)

He's a Royal Prince Charming
who spells his laughter and love
around his friends;
especially on his female darlings.

For him, today matters a lot
very optimistic for every event in action
or in his thought.

He treats love as an adventure
Dealing with his affairs is not so easy;
to lure him away with another partner.
Flirting and venturesome are his two equations
Meeting new people, celebrating life is his only
right of fundamental.

But living the same routine
meeting the same faces;
everyday same talking
makes his appetite boring and annoying.

Building a new relationship boost his level of energy
he is always pleased to begin something
Which keeps his spirit high and moving.

Repetition always bores him
no matter what?

He will continuously pursue new things
With a quiet smile; upon his lips.

Being over-friendly and flirty
It's tough to guess
Has he been in love?
Or were you creating your heart into the mess?

Saggi guy loves to party and get social
always have dared to accept any kind of proposal.
He is a boon to his friends
when he is around for them,
for him,
the spirit of friendship can never end.

He is the innocent and diverse lover
as time passes by, he indeed discovers.

Kindness is his art for him
is too precise in every part.
No matter what,
even if he fails or swims.

He knows for a fact that life is concise
So he believes in living his every day.
Every moment has to be experienced to the fullest,
targeting higher into the sky with his arrow.

Where he can justify his dreams and
desires up to the mark in smoothest.

SAGITTARIUS WOMAN

(Free spirit)

She enjoys life to the fullest
she is the free spirit who will
be spotted as most fabulous.

She is aware of her limits
either in friendship or in high mood spirits.
She likes to have fun and try new things
She hates;
been criticized even if the lights are dim.

A Sagittarius woman is very optimistic
she grew differently;
in her idealistic.
Usually, she is very calm and composed
She loves to hang out with friends in symphonies
of overdosed.

She continues to be everyone's best friend
and maybe the best girlfriend of many.
Once her bonding turns into friendship,
she likes to be close right through the end.

She is entirely free to make her own choices
She is a girl who lives according to her beliefs and
hear her melodious voices.

Being a dynamic personality
She enjoys the opportunities along her way.
She is known as the seeker of truth;
always in urge to explore
flashy rosy with a fresh Ruth.

She is a woman with an open-minded
always fascinated to learn about
religion, morality, philosophy;
and love to be continuously updated.

She is the person where she can't stop digging
herself in deep.
She is the calm personality
like a lazy cat who loves to sleep.

She is ruled by the Jupiter planet
when she loses her cool.

She only yells, 'Dammit.'

She never lingers in one place for too long
If you want to be with her,
you have to sing with her along.

Sagittarius is an excellent reader,
If they are not reading the book, then definitely they are reading you.

CAPRICORN

CAPRICORN

(Symbol: Goat)

Dec 22–Jan 20

C – Consistent
A – Ambitious
P – Patience
R – Reputed
I – Incredible
C – Classy
O – Organized
R – Responsible
N – Never give-up

CAPRICORN

(Serious & Independent)

The earth is my element
It's not easy messing with my temperament.
Saturn is my dominating planet which accords me,
the uniqueness of patience and magnet.

It is difficult for everyone to understand
the nature of my heart.
I am always ready to give in love
whether I am near or apart.

Like my crest is a goat
That's why I love to hike through life.
For the freshness and cleanliness to benefit from,
to strive for success and happiness.

My boundaries mean a lot to me
to unlock my limitations.
'Respect' is the only key where I can't figure out,
Either it's good for you,
or it's good for my imagination.

My emotions run very profoundly in silence
without ideas and violence.
Underneath am a thin layer of frozen
in which the waves of patience flow deep within.

I always seem independent and tough
But I have such a craving for emotion.
Yes, my heart is gold
Hard work and forbearance are the only things,
create my personality in the hold.

I am intensely motivated
and highly optimistic about success.
I believe in working hard for a stable future,
as my only eyes always gaze on my success picture.

I am a Capricorn,
I am Classy,
I don't follow trends if,
I find them crazy.

There are times when I get too serious
And sometimes, I am also imperious.
If you believe in taking me for granted,
You will not be easily forgiven or forgotten.

My forbearance and perseverance
is highly admirable.
If I fall once,
I make sure not to repeat the
same nonsense.

CAPRICORN MAN

(Overly Ambitious, Mature Sea-Goat)

He builds a wall around himself
only a few people have access to peep inside
his deep dark shell.

He is conservative
but he,
believes in actions more than words.
Protecting his emotions is his
priority,
remaining practical in every aspect is his quality.

His personality is deep
His intelligence is unique
He chooses his words very carefully,
whenever he decides to speak.

If given a chance, he would come out as a
best leader.
Due to his high work ethics and
his lovely hardworking nature.

His energy is always motivated to
work better and reach extremes.
He aims to go higher, even in his
profound dreams.

Sometimes he acts stubborn,
Sometimes he is pessimistic,
mostly because he takes time
with people;
to open up his mind and
groom himself to be optimistic.

His fun-loving side only his closed ones can see
as he knows very well where he likes to be.

He is generally very hard working
and mature type guy.
Coming across his love book;
you will find him a bit shy.

It's hard for him to be romantic
but he knows the value of a relationship.
It just takes the right person to see his
true emotions,
where his soft side is rarely visible.

CAPRICORN LADY

(Ambitious Sea-Goat)

Capricorns girls are the sunshine
She is blended with a small hurricane.
So many things she doesn't realize
It's also *OKAY* to make people happy sometimes!

She is the old soul born with the
deepest wisdom.
She always knows better when to
talk in her kingdom.

Her inner drive is strong to
accomplish more incredible things.
Being loyal and reliable, she is
always in her full circle of swings.

Practical and rational, she sees
things for what they are.
Traditions are her feelings of pride,
sometimes she pushes too far.

Ms Capricorn may not always be
utterly gorgeous on the outside,
but it may be beautiful inside.

She is serious but not boring
Only she needs the right guy to
to shower his love on her
and keep his patience pouring.

It needs the courage to get into her thick shell
and a calm ear only to listen to her inner yells.

As an earth sign,
her love is much grounded.
But her choice is too branded.

Sometimes it makes her too bossy
which is not good at all.
She ruins her good terms or relations
into messy or saucy.

She is an alpha female
Amazingly hard and loves to analyse details.

She will weather any storm
Disappointment or tragedy?
She knows very well,
how to rise upwards in reality.

Saving not only for rainy days,
but also keeping in mind.

The factor,
to survive her retirement in about 50 unique ways.

Give too much thought to the future
she loves to save money as a strong protector.

♑

Capricorns love smart people by nature,
Not by diplomas.

AQUARIUS

AQUARIUS

(Symbol: Water Bearer)

Jan 20–Feb 18

A – Air Element
Q – Quick Thinker
U – Unpredictable
A – Altruistic
R – Rebellious
I – Intellectual
U – Unconventional
S – Stubborn

AQUARIUS

(Free-Spirited & Imaginative)

I am born between
January and February.
So I am a little touchy and
sometimes turns my days into
'merry' or 'solitary'.

I am born reserved and quiet
but on the other hand, my thoughts are
eccentric and bright.

I am known as a deep thinker
and highly intelligent too, who
loves to support others
in all directions from black to blue.

I see the things without being bias
I am not a personality of judging,
the book by its covers from getting scared of any virus.

I see the place of the universe with
full of possibilities.
In my world, there is always a
chance of never-ending
opportunities.

I am a little shy as being ruled by the planet
Uranus,

with imaginative attributes that make me
complete Aquarius.

I am always thrilled to
predict my future.
I know perfectly,
what I will do
even after five or ten decades from my built-in structure.

Uranus gives me the ability to
change rapidly.
Rapid thinking is like a click of a finger
even if others always surround me.

The emblem of Aquarius
Is the,
bearer of water.
I lavish the world with my reflection
and fresh ideas.
In the same way,
as the water bearer carries
like valuable cash offered to others.

I am open-minded and
I think very differently.
I, too, have an innovative
attitude,
I pride myself in art only to
express my,
mystical mood.

Sometimes it is hard to guess
What will I do next?
I am unpredictable
that
it makes me quite comfortable.

Meeting new people
Exploring new places
Drawn towards photography and arts,
with people, it makes me well connects.

For the most part
I am not a judgmental sign.
You have your way well
I have mine.

Science and Philosophy quite
interest me,
As am always in search of the
answers in such kinds of mysteries.

Like my symbol, the water bearer
I wish to allow the world
to benefit from my wisdom.
Strong beliefs and fixed opinions
are outside of my system.

I remain calm and peaceful
I do not lose my temper quickly.
Having an introverted personality,
I don't open up to others
easily.

Friends and acquaintances are too many
A hidden artist is inside me.
Writing, Drawing, Crafting
Oh! Let it be,
I can pick up any.

Rebellious and stubborn,
I can't live without it.

Some consider me quickly and weird
but I am proud of myself to be.

AQUA MAN

(Let's revolutionize things with experiments)

Aquarius Man is very unpredictable
Just like the airflow,
It is his key element.
He truly believes in shuffling,
between here and there.

He wants to hide his emotions
from everybody.
But internally, he deeply
needs to speak to somebody.

For Aquarius men, all the
the person he meets has
a special place in his heart.
Everyone for him is unique and
no one loves to stay far apart.

Egoism is not one of his
personality traits.
He likes open-minded partners
to speak up endlessly; from various corners,
even though if some exist in space.

The ruler is the planet Uranus
Thus always in the mood for various
experiments.
He carries the same thing

in his love life too.
It needs little hard work to keep him
stable;
for such a long time with you.

Only on this,
don't judge him wrong at heart.
It's just his nature to look for
new things,
where his soulful spirit sings and dances apart.

Once he falls in love,
he is a great shout out to his partners.
He is the guy by bringing pleasures
and reassures others.

He walks through veils in various shades of colours
He is the man of his partner, a sympathetic lover.

He loves his space but always
makes time for his special people.
Hard to read, but easy to love,
like walking with him on the clouds above.

He is a man of two extreme moods
He is either black or white
without sounding rude.

He has no grey colour within;
Aqua man can be close to you
Or you may find detached from him.

His personality sways between
being friendly and ignored.
He can be insensitive sometimes
for not being sure of his feelings,
between his happy lines.

He is a great communicator
thus,
he has a lot of friends and suitor.

Everyone enjoys singing his praises.
Aqua Man keeps writing poetry
for all ages.

AQUA WOMAN

(Keep trying to understand her)

She is a Paradox
She is Faithful and
yet detached.
She is Committed
and, yet, relaxed.

She loves everyone
and yet no one.
She is sociable
but also unpredictable.

She is gentle
Yet too, though.
She is passionate but
she can also be
platonic.

She is tough to handle
But seems,
Somewhere easily can be manageable.

She is water
Powerful enough to drown you
Soft enough to cleanse you and,
deep enough to save you.

Her thoughts are like out of the box

full of glitter with blue-chip stocks.
Her lifestyle to live life on the edge,
sometimes soft on the sand or sometimes
hugging the hedge.

She may not be the compassionate listener
But certainly, you can call,
whenever you need her.

She is the woman of free spirits
She loves to be with her friends,
and be in her complete appearance.

She lives in a beautiful balance
refusing to let stress or
negativity overcomes her.

She's a homemaker
who knows how to take care
of her man.

But most of all
she's independent,
she knows
how to take care of herself.

Aqua woman is a kind of riddle
she is very autonomous and
highly unpredictable.
When she is sad and wants
to cry,
she will wear a smile on her face
like seeing a pudding and pie.

She is a treasure chest of
sugar, spice and
everything nice.
She believes in spreading
happiness,
to make her world paradise.
It is precisely not hard to impress her
as she appreciates all the
little things in life.
But if you hurt her, she won't forget you
easily,
none of the sorry would work too evenly.

Aqua woman is the exciting blend of
mischief and deep thoughts.

You can't bottle the four winds in the box
or tie the clouds together,
while bouncing with chains or struggling with locks.

She is the air sign she will roam freely
whenever she feels, and wherever she is
welcomed easily.

Aquarius is naturally curious and loves, to ask a lot of questions.

PISCES

PISCES

(Symbol: Two Fishes)

Feb 19–Mar 20

P – Perfectionist
I – Idealistic
S – Selfless
C – Creative
E – Empathetic
S – Spontaneous

PISCES

(Emotional & Spiritual)

Like a fish in the water
I go with the flow,
I count each move of mine
Step by step, something slow.

Swimming upstream is a complete
waste of energy.
Let the universe carry me and
trust my institution.
As am okay,
to keep a watch in my inclination.

I am notoriously difficult to define
My personality cannot be
pinned down.
As I like very much to get admired
and adored,
if there are beautiful people around.

I complete the circle and refresh
the wheel of the Zodiac.
Two fishes swimming in
opposite directions in spite,
of various distractions.

My emblem has the meaning of its own
Despite being in contrary directions;

we are joined together with extreme
affections.

The thread of life reminds us that
we can never separate.
We have a bond as
there is no time for hate.

My empathy and emotions are
unfathomably deep.
I hug mysteries and create the universe
while every Zodiac sleeps.

I communicate with strange and
magical creatures.
With my remarkable imaginations,
I give my life simple, unique visions.

I am the architect of my dream world,
where I am in a mystical trance.
My fantasizes turns into poetry
And,
my feelings into music and arts.

I love the depth of compassion and
empathy.
I am a spiritual lover who is
devoted to unconditional love and
divinity.

Being the last sign of the Zodiac
I possess some characteristics of
all the 12 signs exact.

I am not someone who takes orders very well
I prefer to work in isolation and run
my life in my way,
or sometimes it can be Hell to me,
or sometimes it can be Heaven.

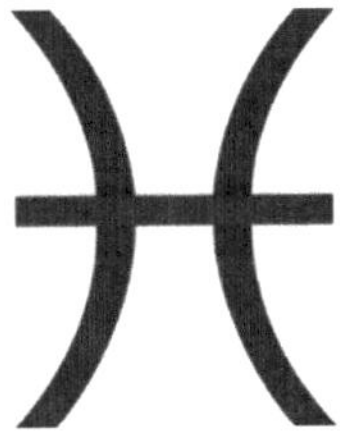

PISCES GUY

(Most Sensible & Sensitive Ones)

Pisces is the last zodiac sign, and
that's why it is considered the oldest among all.
Being a mutable water sign
has a powerful sixth sense above all.

Pisces Man personality
has a touch of femininity.

Only because of the extreme gentle care
he is always available for his loved ones.
In every place,
In every situation
Just call him,
You will find him there.

He needs to reassure of your love
all the time.
He delights her lover with love and gifts,
as the nights grow longer and the seasons' shifts.

He absorbs tons of emotions.
But he can't have,
various sides in various situations.

He likes to feel like a
'Saviour'
As he never judges people,
with their behaviour.

He has the ability
to imagine his intentions into
reality.
He can be a good leader,
But
often stay away from
responsibilities.

He does well in jobs which
includes brainstorming.
He is also an outstanding thinker
like an out of the box.
He can drop anything because his mind is like a fox.

A Pisces Man in love is the best thing to see.
He can climb to any heights
to show his love as '*you*' wanted to be.

He is the man to believe in
action and words.
He adores his relationship like an
Sacred;
who loves to hear,
the morning and evening birds.

A Pisces Man is a natural healer,
he can take his partners out
from any reverie.

The kind of love he can offer
can make you believe in love;
to a whole other level of being together.

He is a man of a high level of patience
It is hard for him to say '*no*' in
any situations.

He is like a still water
deep and silent.
Sometimes he can act like flowing water
without the mood swings or,
without any turbulence.

MERMAID PISCES

(Sea Goddess)

She is mysterious
She is sensual
She is too romantic
She is also spiritual.

Her dreams are vivid
Her sense is profound
Any human cannot easily
understand,
she overflows along with the
sound.

She believes in kindness and oneness
She loves magic and fragrances,
plenty of boxes of romances.

She's lovely, gentle and feminine
Her feeling is a sense of adrenaline.
Mermaid Queen is very captivating and
fascinating.
The ultimate enchantress,
she will simply disappear instead of
confronting.

She needs a man to complete
protect her and nourish her.
Make her feel as if she's required,
like rich and wise, in silk and fur.

She needs patience and sympathy
he has to be gentle with her.
Don't poke her for fun and,
accept her harshly.

Like rivers and seas
Piscean woman swims
Intense and highly.
She rules by Neptune, which
gives her the power exceptionally.

She's great with friends and strangers.
Every person is always dealt with warmly,
even if they are an outgoing greeter.

She would like to pursue a profession
where she can fulfil her dreams.
She is imaginative with highly
sensitive beings.

Romance and the Piscean woman
is like a summer storm.
When it comes to love,
she gives everything in warm.

She is receptive to others
people needs.
In a world of takers, she is truly
a giver,
even if she fails or succeeds.

She is water.
Deep enough to save you,
soft enough to cleanse you
Be aware.
She is also,
powerful enough to drown you.

♓

Pisces do not get
Angry,
They get Cold.

Hashtags of Your Zodiac:

LIBRA

#DecisionsDecisions

SCORPIO

#LoyaltyIsEarned

SAGITTARIUS

#IAmASecretReader

CAPRICORN

#GottaMakeTheMoney

AQUARIUS

#LOLAmUnpredictable

PISCES

#IAmNotMadIAmthinking

The Most Compatible Signs

ARIES: Gemini, Sagittarius, Leo, Aquarius
TAURUS: Capricorn, Pisces, Virgo, Cancer
GEMINI: Aquarius, Libra, Aries, Leo
CANCER: Pisces, Taurus, Scorpio, Virgo
VIRGO: Taurus, Capricorn, Cancer, Pisces
LIBRA: Gemini, Aquarius, Leo, Sagittarius
SCORPIO: Pisces, Cancer, Capricorn, Libra
SAGITTARIUS: Aries, Libra, Leo, Cancer
CAPRICORN: Virgo, Taurus, Scorpio, Pisces
AQUARIUS: Gemini, Sagittarius, Libra, Aries
PISCES: Cancer, Scorpio, Taurus, Capricorn

CELESTIAL FACTS ABOUT ZODIAC

CANCER and LEO are the only signs of the Zodiac, dominated by skylights – the Sun and the Moon. In astrology, they represent a husband and a wife and are the Zodiac King and Queen.

The constellation SAGITTARIUS, the archer, is among the first to be identified.

According to Zoroaster, the new Star that appeared when Jesus was born was part of the constellation of VIRGO, the maiden or unmarried woman.

As an array of scales, LIBRA is the only sign of the Zodiac represented by an inanimate object.

Healers who counsel their patients based on knowledge of the Zodiac say that people born under the sign of PISCES should avoid alcohol.

References:

55 Fascinating Facts about the Zodiac
55 Fascinating Facts about the Zodiac | FactRetriever

STAY IN TOUCH

Readers are my Strength

Lovely Star Readers,

Here comes my third poetic journey with all of you. As I mentioned, I am not an astrologist or a tarot card reader. I only wrote these poems because I felt there had to be something for our Astro Signs. After all, we all belong to some of these signs. Understanding personalities is a necessity in every connection.

I hope everyone has enjoyed reading about you and your beloved Astro in the poetic form.

I am no more lonely on this journey; like your love, responses are making my trip more exciting and productive. There is no single day where I don't think about my known and unknown readers wherever they are in this corner of the planet earth.

I had a lovely unique feeling while writing these poems for YOU and ME.

If you love a book, never hesitate to tell the author. Your reviews might just arrive on a day when they feel like giving up on writing.

Thank you so much for your lovely read. I know there are many books out to choose from at your fingertip, and it means a lot for me that you picked up one of mine and decide to spend your valuable time reading it.

Review this, R*eviews even a minor one, are a massive support to a rising author. If you enjoyed the book and didn't mind sharing your opinions, please consider leaving a review on Amazon.in or Amazon.com, Flipkart, Goodreads, Evincepub Store. The book is* *available on Kindle, Google Books, Google Playstore, and Evincepub E-Store in an ebook format.*

Share this. When *you share this book on social media, you're getting more people to discover this story. And word-of-mouth is the best marketing for the budding author.*

Connect with me as you have always been doing. *I'd love to hear from you!*

You all are always welcome to visit on:

www.theauthorsrk.com
My Instagram id: authorsrk
YouTube Channel: mUcH LoVe Author SRK!

May the stars of heaven sparkle with love and laughter in your life.

Thank you & Stay Bless!

- Shaheen Kazi

Read more at Evincepub by Shaheen Kazi

What happens when your first love is seventeen years older than you?

Age Was… Just a Number

Pages: 348
Format: Paperback/Kindle
Language: English
Subject: Fiction/Romance
ISBN-10: 9390197597
ISBN-13: 978-9390197590

A collection of various shades of 30 Romantic Poems. Cupids Arrow is a colourful bouquet with various fragrances of love.

Cupids Arrow

Pages: 95
Format: Paperback/Hardcover/Kindle
Language: English
Subject: Poetry
ISBN-10: 9390442850
ISBN-13: 978-9390442850

Here is the book for children's and their parents too, a book of 16 short stories with colourful illustrations; did I mention it has short poems?

BaabuBrown and His School Holidays Vol: 1

Pages: 80
Format: Hardcover/Kindle
Language: English
Subject: Children's & Young Adult
ISBN-10: 9354460909
ISBN-13: 978-9354460906